Alcohol

Understanding Words in Context

Curriculum Consultant: JoAnne Buggey, Ph.D.
College of Education, University of Minnesota

By Carol O'Sullivan

Greenhaven Press, Inc.
P.O. Box 289009
San Diego, CA 92198-0009

Titles in the opposing viewpoints juniors series:

Smoking   Death Penalty
Gun Control   Drugs and Sports
Animal Rights   Toxic Wastes
AIDS   Patriotism
Alcohol   Working Mothers
Immigration   Terrorism

Cover photo: J. Tesson/H. Armstrong Roberts

Library of Congress Cataloging-in-Publication Data

Alcohol : understanding words in context / [edited] by Carol
   O'Sullivan ; curriculum consultant, JoAnne Buggey.
       p.   cm. — (Opposing viewpoints juniors)
     Summary: Presents opposing viewpoints on three aspects of alcohol
   and alcoholism.
     ISBN 0-89908-634-9
     1. Alcoholism—Juvenile literature.   2. Drinking of alcoholic
   beverages—Juvenile literature.   3. Advertising—Alcoholic
   beverages—Juvenile literature.   4. Critical thinking—Juvenile
   literature.   5. Word recognition—Juvenile literature.
   [1. Alcohol.   2. Alcoholism.]   I. O'Sullivan, Carol, 1945–
   II. Buggey, JoAnne.   III. Series.
   HV5066.A4 1989
   362.29′2—dc20   89-11712
                                                                    CIP
                                                                    AC

CONTENTS

An Introduction to Opposing Viewpoints

When people disagree, it is hard to figure out who is right. You may decide one person is right just because the person is your friend or a relative. But this is not a very good reason to agree or disagree with someone. It is better if you try to understand why these people disagree. On what main points do they differ? Read or listen to each person's argument carefully. Separate the facts and opinions that each person presents. Finally, decide which argument best matches what you think. This process, examining an argument without emotion, is part of what critical thinking is all about.

This is not easy. Many things make it hard to understand and form opinions. People's values, ages, and experiences all influence the way they think. This is why learning to read and think critically is an invaluable skill. Opposing Viewpoints Juniors books will help

you learn and practice skills to improve your ability to read critically. By reading opposing views on an issue, you will become familiar with methods people use to attempt to convince you that their point of view is right. And you will learn to separate the authors' opinions from the facts they present.

Each Opposing Viewpoints Juniors book focuses on one critical thinking skill that will help you judge the views presented. Some of these skills are telling fact from opinion, recognizing propaganda techniques, and locating and analyzing the main idea. These skills will allow you to examine opposing viewpoints more easily.

Each viewpoint in this book is paraphrased from the original to make it easier to read. The viewpoints are placed in a running debate and are always placed with the pro view first.

Understanding Words in Context

Whenever you read, you may come across words you do not understand. Sometimes, because you do not know a word or words, you will not fully understand what you are reading. One way to avoid this is to interrupt your reading and look up the unfamiliar word in the dictionary. Another way is to examine the unfamiliar word in context. That is, by studying the words, ideas, and attitudes that surround the unfamiliar word, you can often determine its meaning.

In this Opposing Viewpoints Juniors book, you will be asked to determine the meaning of words you do not understand by considering their use in context.

Sometimes a word that has the same meaning as the unfamiliar word will be used in the sentence or in a surrounding sentence. This word will alert the reader to the meaning of the unfamiliar word. An example is:

Many animal species are **endangered** by human activities. Their lives are threatened by people destroying the environment.

The unfamiliar word is **endangered.** The clue is the word *threatened.* The second sentence is an explanation of how people are endangering animals. It is relating the same idea as the first sentence, but it is a little more specific. So, the words threatened and endangered should mean about the same thing. In fact, they do.

LOOK AT SURROUNDING SENTENCES

Often, the surrounding sentences will not contain a word similar to the unfamiliar word. They may, however, contain ideas that suggest the meaning of the unknown word. An example is:

The United States has many **assets.** It has beautiful scenery, natural resources, generous people, and great wealth.

The meaning of the word **assets** can be determined by studying the ideas around it. Beautiful scenery, natural resources, generous people, and great wealth are all desirable things to have. Therefore, assets must mean things that are desirable to own.

In some cases, words and ideas that have opposite meanings can offer the reader clues about an unfamiliar word. For example:

Seldom will you find a man with more than one wife. Most men are **monogamous.**

The unfamiliar word is **monogamous.** The clue is *more than one wife* in the first sentence. In this case, a contrast between the first and second sentence is used. The author of this sentence is saying, "You do not usually find this, so you do usually find that," or "You do not usually find a man with more than one wife, so you do usually find a man with only one wife." Monogamous, then, must mean "having only one wife."

DIFFICULT WORDS

Sometimes the meanings of unfamiliar words are more difficult to determine. You just have to pay attention to the meaning of the sentence to figure them out. Here is an example:

Pickpockets can be **incapacitated** by cutting off their hands.

To determine what **incapacitated** means, you first have to figure out what cutting off pickpockets' hands would accomplish. It would stop them from picking people's pockets. So incapacitated must mean that a person is unable to do something.

In many cases, you will not be able to determine what a word means by its use in the sentence. You will have to look it up in the dictionary. Consider the following example:

The crowd gathered in the auditorium. I noticed that everyone looked **pensive.** I wondered what was happening.

In this case, the meaning of **pensive** cannot be determined by its use in the sentence or paragraph. There is not enough information. It could mean *anxious, happy, different, sad,* or *ridiculous.* It means *thoughtful.*

STUDYING THE CONTEXT

In the following viewpoints, several of the words are highlighted. These words might be unfamiliar to you. You should be able to determine the meanings of these highlighted words by studying them in context—that is, by using the surrounding words and ideas to determine the meaning of the word. As you read the material presented in this book, then, stop at the unfamiliar words and see if you can determine their meanings.

Finally, use a dictionary to see how well you have understood the words in context.

FIGURE OUT THE WORD'S MEANING

We asked two students to give their opinions on the alcohol issue. We asked them to look up some unfamiliar words and use them in sentences. But they had to use these words in such a way that the reader could determine their meanings. Try to figure out the meanings of the words you do not understand by studying them in context. Check your dictionary to see if you are right.

I believe it's all right to drink alcohol.

People should be allowed to drink if they want to. After all, drinking isn't illegal. And it isn't a sin either. The Bible tells stories about people drinking wine.

Sure, some people drink alcohol all the time. Their lives are pretty worthless. But these people are **habitual** drinkers. They can't live without the stuff. Most people drink alcohol because they like it, not because they have to have it. They can take it or leave it.

Both my parents have a drink or two when they come home from work. They have jobs that make them uptight sometimes. They come home irritated. But after a couple of drinks, they're much nicer to be around.

Drinking is like everything else. It's okay as long as you don't overdo it. People who want to make other people stop drinking are on some kind of weird **crusade.** They just want people to do everything their way.

I don't think anybody should drink alcohol.

People do stupid things when they drink. One **idiotic** thing they do is drink and drive a car. Everyone thinks it's wrong to drink and drive when they haven't been drinking. But when people get drunk, they forget about all the things they think are wrong. It seems that the more **inebriated** people become, the more they forget what's right and wrong.

Also, I don't think alcohol is good for you. It makes you sick. Anything that makes you sick can't be good for you.

One time my big brother took me on a camping trip and let me drink two beers. I was so sick I had to stay in the tent all day. It's just not worth it to have a good time for a couple of hours and then be sick all day.

Tim and Heidi have very different opinions about drinking. Both of them use words in their arguments that you might not understand. But you should be able to determine the meanings of these words by considering their use in context.

Tim:

Sure, some people drink alcohol all the time. But these people are **habitual** drinkers. They can't live without the stuff.

NEW WORD	CLUE WORD OR IDEA	DEFINITION
habitual	drink alcohol all the time	doing something all the time because you have a habit of doing it and cannot stop

Heidi:

When people get drunk, they forget about all the things they think are wrong. It seems that the more **inebriated** people become, the more they forget what's right and wrong.

NEW WORD	CLUE WORD OR IDEA	DEFINITION
inebriated	drunk	drunk

You should be able to figure out the meanings of the words *crusade* and *idiotic* by their use in context. What do these words mean?

Both Tim and Heidi think they are right about drinking. Which student do you think is right? Why?

As you continue to read through the viewpoints in this book, keep a list of the new words you learn and include the definitions of these words.

CHAPTER 1

PREFACE: Is Alcohol Always Harmful?

Drinking alcoholic beverages is popular in the United States. For many people, drinking a couple of cocktails before lunch and dinner and serving wine with meals is considered normal. Having a few drinks while sitting around with friends is all part of having a good time.

But alcohol can contribute to bad as well as good times. People who drink too much often lose control of their lives. They sometimes lose their jobs because they cannot perform at work while under the influence of alcohol. Sometimes they become violent and destroy property or hurt other people. Also, when people drink, they do not realize that their eyes, muscles, and reflexes do not work as well as when they have not been drinking. Too often these people try to drive automobiles. The result is sometimes injury or death.

Because of the problems alcohol can cause, many people believe drinking alcoholic beverages is always a bad idea. These people admit that it may be difficult to avoid alcohol, especially at parties and other social activities. But they advise people to request non-alcoholic beverages at these social gatherings. They insist that other party guests will respect the person who is brave enough to ask for ginger ale.

On the other hand, some people argue that reasonable amounts of alcohol can be good for you. In fact, statistics show that people who drink some alcohol live longer than people who never drink. Some psychologists and sociologists think this may be partly because people who drink are more social, more involved in activities, and enjoy life more than people who do not drink. These psychologists and sociologists believe people who enjoy life live longer than people who do not enjoy life.

Some people, including many doctors, think people who drink may live longer because drinking relaxes the body. This relaxation can prevent stress-related illnesses such as heart attacks and high blood pressure.

While reading these viewpoints, decide if you think the benefits outweigh the problems of drinking alcohol.

Drinking alcohol in moderation can be healthy

> **Editor's Note:** This viewpoint is paraphrased from an article by William J. Darby. Dr. Darby is president of the Nutrition Foundation in New York and an emeritus professor of biochemistry at Vanderbilt University School of Medicine. In this viewpoint, Dr. Darby claims that drinking a reasonable amount of alcohol not only makes life pleasant but also reduces the threat of heart attack and high blood pressure. Remember to try to figure out the meaning of the highlighted words by their use in context. Guidelines are not included in the margins for four highlighted words in this viewpoint. These words are included in the Critical Thinking Skill at the end of the chapter.

Most people enjoy a few drinks during the day. American business-people look forward to their martinis at lunch. The French consider a bottle of wine an essential part of a meal. In nearly every country of the world, alcoholic beverages serve an important social function.

In America, the attitude toward drinking has **vacillated** between two extremes. On the one hand, people believe that drinking is a sin. On the other hand, they believe it is an all-American activity. The middle ground has been neglected.

Whether people view drinking as sinful or all-American, they often worry about the effects of drinking. They believe, incorrectly, that reasonable amounts of alcohol, or even a little alcohol, is harmful. They think **moderate** drinking causes the same health problems as too much drinking.

But studies now indicate that drinking moderate amounts of alcohol is good for you. Statistics show that moderate drinkers live longer than **teetotalers**, who never drink, and people who drink too much.

Part of the reason for this **longevity** is that drinkers usually lead active social lives. They also have hobbies they enjoy. Active people usually live longer than inactive people.

But this longevity may be due to other factors as well. A recent study offers evidence that moderate drinking may prevent heart attacks. This study included 464 patients who had been hospitalized with heart attacks. A large number of these heart attack patients were teetotalers. A smaller number were alcohol drinkers.

Between two extremes **gives you a clue to the meaning of** *vacillated.* **The sentence suggests that attitudes toward drinking move between two opposite ideas.** *Vacillate* **means** *to swing* **or** *to sway back and forth.*

In this sentence, *who never drink* **is the clue to the meaning of** *teetotalers.*

Live longer **is the clue to** *longevity. Longevity* **means** *a long life.*

Another study was done in which the case histories of 120,000 patients were considered. This study found that moderate alcohol users were 30 percent less likely to have heart attacks than were teetotalers. The study also showed that people who drank from two to six drinks daily had fewer heart attacks than people who **abstained** from drinking.

In another research project done in Massachusetts, 399 heart attack patients were studied. Results indicated that people who drank even more than six drinks a day had fewer heart attacks than teetotalers.

Besides preventing heart attacks, drinking alcohol may help save people from high blood pressure.

Dr. Arthur Klatsky, a heart specialist in Oakland, California, tested eighty-four thousand men and women. He found that those people who drank two or fewer drinks a day had lower blood pressure than did teetotalers.

Research has shown that drinking alcohol in moderation can be **beneficial** to your health. But now we have the problem of deciding how many drinks are considered moderate. There is evidence that a daily intake of as much as six ounces of liquor, twenty ounces of table wine, or four and one-half bottles of beer causes little, if any, damage to healthy people. But a safe guess is that three drinks a day is moderate.

On the basis of current evidence, we may conclude that moderate use of alcohol is safe. It contributes to our supply of energy and our enjoyment of life. And it may even contribute to our health. So there may be truth to the traditional French toast "à votre santé"—"to your health." And, as some people say, "I'll drink to that."

The clue to *abstained* is a word you just learned, *teetotalers.* Teetotalers are people who do not drink, so *abstain* means to avoid doing something.

Try to determine the meaning of *beneficial* in context of what you just read about how alcohol affects the body.

"Most doctors say that heavy drinkers don't live long, yet you see more old drunks than old doctors."

©Sax/Rothco

Can alcohol be good for you?

Dr. Darby claims alcohol may be good for your health. What proof does he offer that this is true? Does his proof convince you that drinking alcohol is good for you? Why or why not?

VIEWPOINT 2 People should not drink alcohol

Editor's Note: This viewpoint is paraphrased from an article by Glenn D. Everett. Mr. Everett is a journalist. In this viewpoint, he discusses why people should not drink alcohol. While reading, try to understand the meaning of the highlighted words.

You learned the meanings of *teetotaler* and *abstain* in the previous viewpoint. What do these words mean?

You should know the meaning of *pressure*. The clue to *peer* is *friends and associates*. What, then, does *peer pressure* mean?

What word or idea gives you a clue to the meaning of *intoxicated*?

I am a **teetotaler. Abstaining** from drinking has sometimes been difficult. I live in a city where people like to drink. The cocktail party is Washington, D.C.'s greatest social institution.

Back in the old saloon days, people were against drinking. But today the opposite is true. Drinking whiskey and gin cocktails is not only acceptable, it is socially demanded. In small towns, the drinker may be frowned upon. But not in the city. In big cities, drinking is considered normal behavior.

How can teetotalers resist **peer pressure** to drink? How can they refuse when their friends and associates encourage them to drink? Let's face it—saying no is not easy.

I think ministers and youth counselors could deal with this problem if they tried. I think our churches could help our young people learn to refuse alcohol. We need to tell our young people entering professions that call for social contact that they will have to face drinking. We must give them good, concrete reasons for abstaining.

Perhaps I can offer some advice. In the first place, people have to make up their own minds whether to drink or not. I made up my mind in college that I was not going to drink.

I know people who did not make this decision. Now they wish they had. A couple of friends of mine were **expelled** from a small church-run college for being drunk and destroying property. They were kicked out because they tore up the library while they were **intoxicated.** For one of my friends, it meant the ruin of a promising law career.

I also knew a congressman's son who was tried by members of the army because he could not stay away from beer. After his trial, he was dismissed from the army. He finally woke up to the fact that he was ruining his life.

The ones who wake up are lucky. Lots of young men and women do not wake up until they are too far down the road of alcoholism to stop.

From what I could see in college, drinking seemed like a stupid thing to do. But then I got a job as a city editor on a small newspaper. My assignments covering the police court convinced me even further that drinking is **asinine.**

I remember a man who had murdered his wife in a drunken rage. I saw him the morning after. When he sobered up, he regretted the horrible deed he had committed. But it was too late.

I also had to write about the accident cases. They would come to court from hospitals in bandages and splints to be charged with drunken driving or manslaughter. They attended their **arraignments** in physical as well as spiritual pain.

Worst of all was the salesman who had run down two young boys on bicycles. One was dead. The other was crippled by a spinal injury. The judge was stern. He ordered the salesman to spend ten years in the state prison.

The truth is that no one has to drink to be sociable. You can explain that you simply do not drink. Just ask for ginger ale. Nobody will **shun** you. Your friends will still associate with you. I do not care what drinkers say—they have an inner respect for people who do not drink. There is a trend in America toward more and more drinking of alcohol. This increase in drinking will be halted only by those who refuse to give in to peer pressure.

I will never forget the day Premier Mendes-France of France attended a meeting where people were drinking. When everyone else raised their glasses of alcohol to make a toast, he raised his glass of milk. He wanted people to know that he no longer **sanctioned** alcohol. He wanted to get the message across that alcohol was destroying his country. Because of this, he no longer approved of drinking. Mendes-France gained the respect of everyone present for having the nerve to refuse alcohol.

The clue to the meaning of *arraignments* is *come to court...to be charged.* What, then, is an *arraignment*?

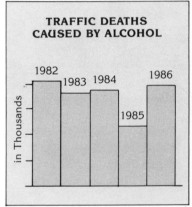

TRAFFIC DEATHS CAUSED BY ALCOHOL

1982 1983 1984 1985 1986

in Thousands

SOURCE: Department of Transportation

What is the clue to the meaning of *sanctioned*? What does *sanctioned* mean?

Should people abstain from drinking alcohol?

Mr. Everett thinks that peer pressure is a major reason people drink. Do you agree? If not, why do you think people drink?

Mr. Everett recommends that ministers and counselors educate young people about alcohol use. Can you think of other people or organizations tht might also be able to inform young people about drinking?

Do you think it's all right to drink alcohol? Why or why not?

Understanding Words in Context

The sentences below come from viewpoints 1 and 2. Try to determine the meaning of each highlighted word by its use in context. Under each sentence or sentences, you will find four definitions for the highlighted word. Choose the one that is closest to your understanding of the word. Use the dictionary to see how well you have understood the words in context.

1. A couple of friends of mine were **expelled** from a small church college for being drunk and destroying property. They were kicked out because they tore up the library while they were intoxicated.

    expelled means:

    a) laughed at
    b) kicked out
    c) fined
    d) put in jail

2. Nobody will **shun** you. Your friends will still associate with you.

    shun means:

    a) hurt
    b) annoy
    c) like
    d) avoid

3. They believe, incorrectly, that reasonable amounts of alcohol or even a little alcohol is harmful. They think **moderate** drinking causes the same health problems as too much drinking.

    moderate means:

    a) elegant
    b) within reasonable limits
    c) forbidden
    d) careless

4. From what I could see in college, drinking seemed like a stupid thing to do. . . . My assignments covering the police court convinced me even further that drinking is **asinine.**

    asinine means:

    a) dumb
    b) funny
    c) religious
    d) essential

CHAPTER 2

PREFACE: Is Alcoholism a Disease?

Alcoholism is a serious problem in the United States. Nearly two hundred thousand people die each year from alcohol abuse. This includes deaths from accidents and diseases caused by alcohol. Also, five thousand babies are born each year with Fetal Alcohol Syndrome. This is a form of mental retardation caused by mothers drinking while pregnant.

While most people admit that alcoholism is a problem, they debate whether alcoholism is a disease.

People who say alcoholism is a disease argue that it has the same qualities and patterns of other diseases. Like many other diseases, it ends in insanity or death. They also claim that alcoholism is probably inherited from one or both of the alcoholic's parents.

But other people argue that alcoholism is not a disease at all. They say that alcoholics drink too much because they like to drink and do not bother to control themselves. These people also say that alcoholics drink because they learned to drink from their parents and their cultures.

When reading these viewpoints, pay attention to which author offers the best evidence about the causes of alcoholism.

Editor's Note: This viewpoint is paraphrased from an article by Mary Ellen Pinkham. Ms. Pinkham is a journalist for *Family Circle* magazine. In this viewpoint, Ms. Pinkham argues that alcoholism is a disease because it is similar to other diseases.

In 1956, the American Medical Association determined that alcoholism is a disease. This was helpful because it meant that an alcoholic could at last get help in a hospital. But it was not helpful in changing the public's opinion that alcoholism is a moral, not a medical, problem. People still think that anyone who drinks too much has no **ethics.** They still tend to **shun** alcoholics.

People think alcoholism is not a disease because it is not like other diseases. They think of a disease as something like the flu that is caused by a germ or virus.

Many doctors, however, believe alcoholism is a disease. They say that it resembles other diseases in some ways. For example, like other diseases, alcoholism is *primary, progressive,* and *chronic.*

By *primary,* doctors mean that alcoholism is a disease by itself. It is not a **symptom** of another illness. It does not indicate some greater social, emotional, or physical problem.

By *progressive,* doctors mean that the problem is going to get worse. In fact, it will lead to insanity or death. The amount of time it takes for an alcoholic to become **demented** or die varies. Sometimes it takes five years. Sometimes it takes fifty. But it will happen. The drinker with the disease of alcoholism will eventually face one of these two fates.

By *chronic,* doctors mean that there is no cure for alcoholism. It can, however, be controlled. With help, an alcoholic may lead a happy, meaningful, and fulfilling life.

What is the clue to the meaning of *ethics*? What does *ethics* mean?

You learned the word *shun* in the previous viewpoint. What does *shun* mean?

What does *symptom* mean? How do you know?

What word provides a clue to the meaning of *demented*? What does *demented* mean?

It is important to understand a few things about the way the disease of alcoholism works in the body. A scientist doing brain research made an interesting discovery. She noticed that the way alcohol affects alcoholics is different from the way it affects non-alcoholics.

She discovered that in the body of normal drinkers, alcohol breaks down into a poisonous substance called *acetaldehyde* (pronounced *as uh 'tal duh hide*). Next it breaks down into carbon dioxide and water. It is then passed off as a waste product.

In alcoholics, the acetaldehyde is not passed off. The alcoholic's body does not produce enough of an enzyme that **eliminates** acetaldehyde, so it remains in the body. (An enzyme is a protein-like substance that is produced by the cells of the body.)

What words or ideas provide clues to *eliminates*? What does this word mean?

"SURE PAL, YOU CAN RIDE ALONG...."

Gary Markelstein. Reprinted with permission.

When acetaldehyde remains in the body, it travels to the brain. There it becomes a powerful narcotic-like substance called THIQ. This substance is present in the brain of an alcoholic drinker. It is not present in the brain of a non-alcoholic drinker.

So an abnormal enzyme is probably responsible for the way an alcoholic's body handles alcohol. This **aberrant** enzyme might be inherited. It might explain why children of alcoholics are three to five times more likely to be alcoholics than the general population.

Beside being a physical disease, alcoholism is also a feeling disease. This means that it affects the alcoholic's emotional life. The range of feelings in the alcoholic **vacillates** from depression to **euphoria**, with normal feelings in the middle.

The feeling disease of alcoholism progresses in stages. In the first stage, drinkers feel euphoria while drinking. After a drinking bout, they feel normal. Also in the first stage, drinkers look forward to having a drink. But they are not too upset if alcohol is unavailable.

In later stages, however, drinkers become hooked on alcohol. They become extremely upset if they cannot find alcohol. They become so **distraught** that they may go to great trouble to get their hands on a drink. And after a drinking bout, they do not feel normal. They feel the emotional pain of guilt, shame, and self-hatred.

If drinkers do not get help, they go into the final stage of alcoholism. People in this stage drink every day, sometimes all day. They feel emotional pain all the time. They drink in an attempt to **alleviate** this pain. They count on alcohol just to make them stop hurting. They are so unhappy they may even try to commit suicide.

Alcoholism is a sad disease. It affects mostly nice, middle-class people who are caring for their families as best they can. Basically, alcoholics are regular folks who happen to have a serious problem. This problem affects every part of their lives. It causes problems in their relationships with family and friends. It also affects their performance at work.

Alcoholics are not bad or immoral. They are suffering from a disease. They are probably unaware that they even have it.

What word provides a clue to *aberrant*? What does *aberrant* mean?

You are familiar with *vacillates*. What does this word mean?

Consider the words and ideas that surround the word *euphoria*. What does this word mean?

What does *distraught* mean? How do you know?

Alleviate can be understood by considering its use in context. What does *alleviate* mean?

THE EFFECTS OF ALCOHOL

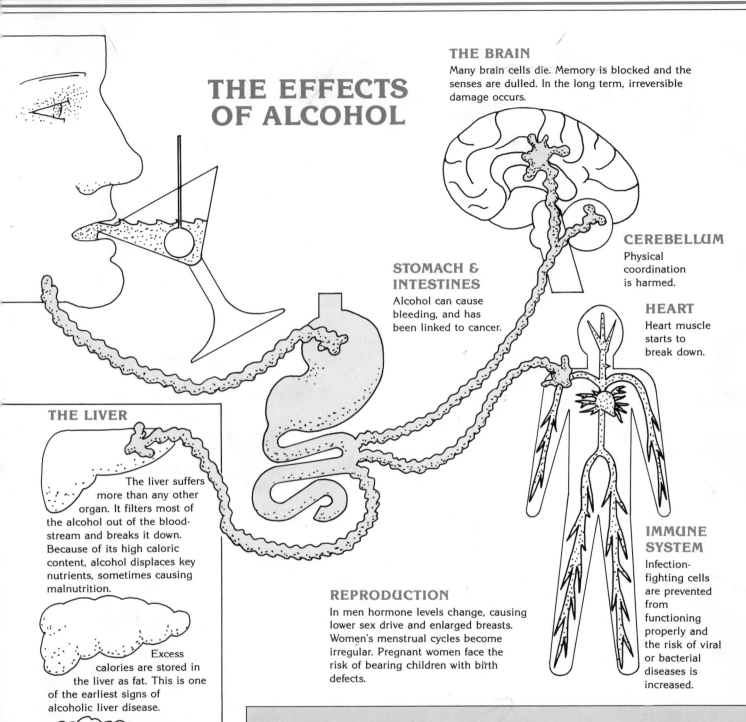

THE BRAIN
Many brain cells die. Memory is blocked and the senses are dulled. In the long term, irreversible damage occurs.

CEREBELLUM
Physical coordination is harmed.

HEART
Heart muscle starts to break down.

STOMACH & INTESTINES
Alcohol can cause bleeding, and has been linked to cancer.

IMMUNE SYSTEM
Infection-fighting cells are prevented from functioning properly and the risk of viral or bacterial diseases is increased.

THE LIVER
The liver suffers more than any other organ. It filters most of the alcohol out of the bloodstream and breaks it down. Because of its high caloric content, alcohol displaces key nutrients, sometimes causing malnutrition.

Excess calories are stored in the liver as fat. This is one of the earliest signs of alcoholic liver disease.

Eventually the liver cells die, resulting in cirrhosis, a degeneration of the organ.

REPRODUCTION
In men hormone levels change, causing lower sex drive and enlarged breasts. Women's menstrual cycles become irregular. Pregnant women face the risk of bearing children with birth defects.

Is alcoholism a disease?

Why does Ms. Pinkham think alcoholism is a disease? What does she mean by *primary, progressive,* and *chronic*?

What does Ms. Pinkham mean when she says alcoholism is a *feeling* disease?

Editor's Note: This viewpoint is paraphrased from an article by Herbert Fingarette. Mr. Fingarette is a philosophy professor at the University of California at Santa Barbara. He argues that alcoholism is not a disease. He says the belief that alcoholism is a disease has been costly both to the public and to the alcoholic.

The notion that alcoholism is a disease is a myth. There is no medical proof that this is true. This lack of proof that alcoholism is a disease should prevent doctors from treating it as a real illness.

People who argue that alcoholism is a disease say that it progresses in stages, as do other illnesses. But alcoholism does not develop in any definite stages. Some alcoholics claim loss of control. Others never do. Some have problems getting along with their friends and family. Others have no such problems. Some eventually become **demented.** Others remain sane.

People who believe alcoholism is a disease claim that the illness is due to an enzyme that is not working properly. In alcoholics, something is wrong with the enzyme needed to **eliminate** acetaldehyde from their bodies. A person who is drinking produces acetaldehyde, a liquid, from the alcohol in his or her system. Because alcoholics cannot eliminate this substance, it goes to the brain and becomes **toxic.** This poisoning of the brain is supposed to be the cause of alcoholism.

But there is absolutely no proof that there is a **causal link** between alcoholism and the presence of acetaldehyde in the brain. In fact, there is a problem with this argument. In order for acetaldehyde to be in the brain, alcohol must be present in the body. Acetaldehyde is made from alcohol.

You learned *demented* and *eliminate* in previous viewpoints. What do these words mean?

The meaning of *toxic* can be determined by studying the words surrounding it. What does *toxic* mean?

What is a *causal link*? How do you know?

How then does this explain why an alcoholic who has not had a drink for a long time suddenly starts **craving** it? There is no alcohol in his or her system to trigger the acetaldehyde that is supposed to cause him or her to have a strong desire for alcohol.

Some people also claim that alcoholism is a **genetic** disease. But this is utterly false. The idea that alcoholism is passed on from generation to generation is based partly on an article by Donald Goodwin. This article states that about 18 percent of the sons of alcoholic parents become alcoholic. Simple arithmetic tells us that if 18 percent of the sons of alcoholics do become alcoholic, 82 percent do not. It seems to me that this is evidence that sons of alcoholics do *not* usually become alcoholics.

It is important that we get rid of the myth that alcoholism is a disease. We are not doing any service to alcoholics by telling them that they have an illness. The message we are sending them is that they are helpless. We are telling them they have an incurable disease that forces them to drink, and they might as well give up efforts to stop.

We need to stop thinking of alcoholism as a disease for another reason. The cost of treating alcoholism is **exorbitant.** In fact, it costs over one billion dollars a year to treat this so-called disease. Health insurance companies have to pay for the treatment of alcoholics as if they had a real disease. This means we have to pay more for our health insurance.

Figure out the meaning of *craving* by studying the words and ideas surrounding *craving.*

What are the clues that help you to understand the meaning of *genetic*? What does this word mean?

What does *exorbitant* mean? How do you know?

Reprinted with special permission of King Features Syndicate, Inc.

In addition, alcoholics get the same benefits at work as employees with real diseases. This includes paid sick leave. Alcoholics also get workmen's compensation. This means they get paid when they get hurt on the job and have to stay home, even if they got hurt because they were drinking.

There is one more danger of calling alcoholism a disease. People tend to blame alcohol for problems the drinker causes. Alcoholics are no longer expected to follow the rules and regulations of society because they are "sick."

People drink for several reasons. They drink because they are frustrated or tense. They drink for excitement and pleasure and because they are tired. Sometimes they drink because they cannot resist **peer pressure.**

You should be familiar with *peer pressure.* You learned it in a previous viewpoint. What does *peer pressure* mean?

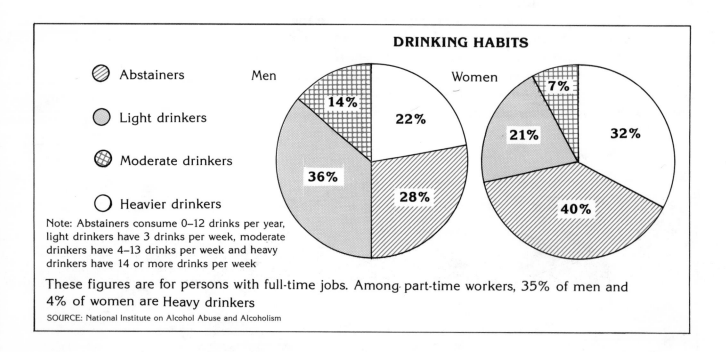

DRINKING HABITS

Abstainers

Light drinkers

Moderate drinkers

Heavier drinkers

Men — 14%, 22%, 36%, 28%

Women — 7%, 21%, 32%, 40%

Note: Abstainers consume 0–12 drinks per year, light drinkers have 3 drinks per week, moderate drinkers have 4–13 drinks per week and heavy drinkers have 14 or more drinks per week

These figures are for persons with full-time jobs. Among part-time workers, 35% of men and 4% of women are Heavy drinkers

SOURCE: National Institute on Alcohol Abuse and Alcoholism

But people do not drink because they have a disease that **compels** them to drink. They are not helpless. They can stop drinking if they want to. We can help them by offering moral support and good advice. We can assist them with their genuine physical ailments. But we have to make it clear that heavy drinkers must take responsibility for their own lives.

Look for clues to the meaning of *compels* in the words and ideas surrounding it. What does *compels* mean?

©1984 USA TODAY. Reprinted with permission.

Can alcoholics control their drinking?

Why does Mr. Fingarette think it is important to stop thinking of alcoholism as a disease? How does he think we can help people who drink too much alcohol?

After reading these two viewpoints about whether alcoholism is a disease, which author did you find most convincing? Why?

Using New Words

Below are six paragraphs that are missing words. Choose the words that best complete the paragraphs from the list of words at the left. The ideas expressed in each paragraph should help you choose the most appropriate word.

symptom
distraught
longevity
eliminate
demented
peer pressure

1. My grandmother has lived a long time. She thinks the reason for her _____ is that she eats healthy food and avoids alcohol.

2. Insanity is a _____ of disease. It is a sign that the drinker suffers from the disease of alcoholism.

3. Some people behave insanely when they drink. Alcohol causes them to become _____.

4. People should _____ alcohol from their diets. Cutting out foods and drinks that are bad for them is the best way to stay healthy.   .

5. Some people drink because of _____. Their friends encourage them to drink.

6. My mother became _____ when she found out that I had been drinking. She was upset because she thinks everyone who drinks is an alcoholic.

CHAPTER 3

PREFACE: **Does Alcohol Advertising Promote Alcoholism?**

The alcohol industry spends around two billion dollars each year advertising its products. Many people claim that because alcoholism is a serious problem in the United States, it is not right to advertise alcoholic beverages. These people claim that the alcohol industry does not mention in its ads that alcohol is habit-forming. And only a few companies that produce alcoholic beverages warn people not to drink too much.

But other people claim that the right to advertise any product is guaranteed by the First Amendment to the Constitution of the United States. This amendment says, in part:

> Congress shall make no law . . . abridging the freedom of speech or of the press.

People who support alcohol advertsing argue that the alcohol industry has the right to say just about anything it wants about its products in its ads. These people also argue that the press has the right to print these ads and that the American people have the right to be informed about the various kinds of alcohol. Therefore, by limiting alcohol advertising, everyone's rights would be taken away.

While reading these two viewpoints, decide if you think the right to free speech in advertising is guaranteed by the First Amendment.

Editor's Note: This viewpoint is paraphrased from an article by Frank McConnell, a professor at the University of California at Santa Barbara. Mr. McConnell is a recovering alcoholic. In the following viewpoint, he claims that alcohol ads attempt to convince people that life is more satisfying with alcohol. He says that the ads do not, however, warn people that alcohol is habit-forming.

What words or ideas provide clues to the meaning of *macho*? What does this word mean?

You learned *sanction* in a previous viewpoint. What does this word mean?

You can determine the meaning of *tolerate* by examining the ideas surrounding it. What does *tolerate* mean?

You learned the word *genetic* in a previous viewpoint. What does it mean?

Who has not seen the commercial, "If you've got the time, we've got the beer?" In it, a group of healthy American males are out for a day of marlin fishing. Or perhaps they are mountain climbing or hang gliding. They are all good buddies just out having a great time. And what do they do at the end of the day? Why, they gather at their favorite bar and start calling for the beer. And they usually do it with a **macho,** he-man American phrase like "Keep 'em coming, Rosie."

Do you know a beer commercial that does not include a group of people? Do you know a wine or liquor ad that shows a lone person drinking? I will answer that for you: You do not.

The makers of these ads purposely include groups of people in them because they want to deliver a specific message. The message is that most people drink. The message tells us that the majority of people in our society not only **tolerate** drinking, they **sanction** it.

Imagine what these ads would be like if heroin were legal. They might show four old pals sitting around the apartment. These old pals might be setting up their spoons, matches, and needles. The ad might say, "This drug's for you."

I am concerned at the way the media inform people that drinking is acceptable. Alcohol is a dangerous substance. And alcoholism is a serious disease. It is a major cause of death in this country. If statistics mean anything, three out of ten of you reading this piece will get this disease. There is evidence that alcoholism is a **genetic** disease, so some of you may already have it.

Alcoholism is also a curious disease. Like tooth decay, it is a disease of civilization. Only when people become civilized enough to turn grain into alcohol and process sugar from cane do illnesses like alcoholism and tooth decay become possible.

I am not saying that people who write the liquor ads are bad people. They are, like the rest of us, just trying to earn a buck. But the ads they write convince us that there is no such thing as alcohol abuse. They make us deny that it is possible to become an alcohol **addict.** The people who write liquor ads want us to ignore the fact that alcohol use can become a habit.

What alcohol ads do sell us is **euphoria.** They make us feel good. They sell us the romantic excitement of a man in a tuxedo and a woman in an evening dress sharing a glass of sherry. Or they sell us the warmth of companionship of ex-football players downing beer after beer. They sell us the pride of success of the wealthy entertainer. She holds her favorite brand of vodka in her hand, praising its clear color. Then she takes a sip and **extols** its smooth, refreshing taste. All these ads make us believe that if we drink that particular brand of alcohol, we too will feel love, companionship, and pride.

I would like to see one of those brandy ads where the dressed-up man and woman drink and have a good time. But I would like the ad to include pictures of the couple the next morning. The pictures would show them sprawled out on the bed, sweaty, dry-mouthed, and sick. This is the real ending to the story about drinking.

What is an *addict*? How do you know?

You have already learned the definition of *euphoria*. What does it mean?

Consider the words and ideas surrounding *extols*. What does this word mean?

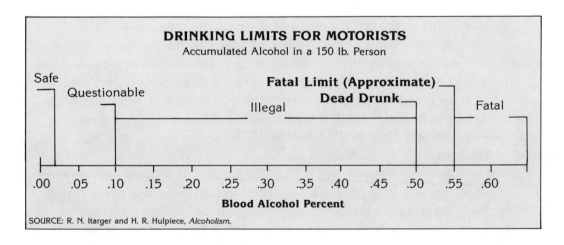

DRINKING LIMITS FOR MOTORISTS
Accumulated Alcohol in a 150 lb. Person

SOURCE: R. N. Itarger and H. R. Hulpiece, *Alcoholism*.

What do alcohol ads sell?

Mr. McConnell says alcohol ads sell "euphoria." What does he mean by this? Do you agree?

Editor's Note: This viewpoint is paraphrased from an article by Clifford Williams, director of government affairs for Miller Brewing Company. Mr. Williams claims that not allowing alcohol advertising would violate the First Amendment to the Constitution of the United States. This amendment guarantees freedom of speech and freedom of the press.

What words or ideas provide clues to *immigrated*? What does it mean?

What does *restrict* mean? How do you know?

What are the *broadcast media*?

You learned the meaning of *causal link* in a previous viewpoint. What does it mean?

What is a *peer group*? How do you know?

America is envied by many people around the world. This is mainly because of the freedoms enjoyed by every American citizen. Freedom to think, freedom to speak, freedom to worship—that is America.

For more than two centuries, millions have **immigrated** to this country. They have come here from their native lands because they want to live in this land of freedom. Those millions come here to practice their beliefs without interference.

But two of our freedoms are being threatened. These are freedom of speech and freedom of the press. These freedoms are guaranteed by the First Amendment to the Constitution. They are being threatened because some groups are trying to get laws passed that **restrict** beer and wine advertising on radio and television. They are trying to limit both the content and the number of these ads on the **broadcast media.**

People who oppose alcohol use say that beer and wine advertising causes drinking problems in this country. But evidence of a **causal link** between alcohol advertising and alcoholism has not been found. This fact was determined in a study by David J. Pittman and M. Dow Lambert of Washington University, St. Louis, Missouri.

There is, however, proof that alcoholism is related to many other factors in a person's life. The state of a person's mind and body help determine whether he or she will develop alcohol problems. A person's **peer group** also influences his or her alcohol use. If a person's friends and associates drink, chances are he or she will too.

There is no proof that stopping or restricting alcohol advertising would prevent alcoholism. Other countries of the world, such as Sweden and the Soviet Union, forbid or restrict alcohol advertising. Yet their people have far greater alcohol problems than Americans do.

Speaking out for a product in a radio or a television ad is a right guaranteed by the First Amendment. **Censoring** beer and wine advertising in the broadcast media is an attack on the rights of all Americans.

Censoring ads is not the answer to responsible drinking. The answer is effective education about the product. Education is the stepping-stone to an informed **consumer.** A consumer who understands the product will use it responsibly. Perhaps he or she will choose not to use it at all.

Miller Lite has been charged with presenting harmful messages to society. But Miller Lite denies these charges. Popular Lite **celebrities** are around fifty years old. These famous people are hardly role models for children and teenagers. Some are former athletes. Others have no association with sports whatsoever. In public appearances, Lite celebrities stress that every person who drinks is responsible for his or her drinking. They also stress that care is necessary when one drives or performs any common tasks that could be dangerous.

Citizens of this country have the freedom to consider information reflecting many viewpoints and beliefs. But to consider this information, they must be able to get hold of it. The right to receive information and the right to provide that information is the foundation of our democracy. Taking away someone else's freedom may mean that our own freedom will be taken away from us.

The meaning of *censoring* can be determined by considering its use in context. What does it mean?

What is a *consumer*? What words or ideas provided the clues?

What are *celebrities*? How do you know?

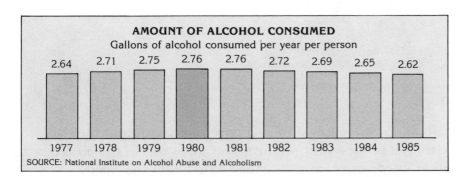

AMOUNT OF ALCOHOL CONSUMED
Gallons of alcohol consumed per year per person

1977	1978	1979	1980	1981	1982	1983	1984	1985
2.64	2.71	2.75	2.76	2.76	2.72	2.69	2.65	2.62

SOURCE: National Institute on Alcohol Abuse and Alcoholism

Does censoring alcohol ads violate freedom of speech?

Do you agree with Mr. Williams that the First Amendment allows freedom of speech in advertising? Do you think alcohol ads should be censored? Why or why not? Do you think ads for any products should be censored? If so, which products?

Understanding Words in Advertising

People try to choose words that best express the ideas they want to communicate to other people. Advertisers, too, choose words they think best express an idea they are trying to communicate to the public about their products. Their purpose is to convince you that you want or need their products.

When reading an ad, you may find words you do not understand. But you may be able to understand these words by considering their use in context. For example, an ad may say "Worthington wool coats are chic. You'll always be well dressed in a Worthington." You might not be familiar with the word *chic* (pronounced *sheek*). But you can guess the meaning of the word by the clue *well dressed. Chic* means *well dressed* or *dressed according to the style.*

A New Taste Explosion

Caribbean WINE COOLER

Lava and water. Out of these basic elements, new land takes shape.

Passion fruit and mango. Out of these delicious fruits, a new wine cooler is created.

The makers of Caribbean Wine Coolers have blended passion fruit and mango to create one exotic new flavor. Enjoy the strikingly different taste of the islands. Experience a creation as rare as a volcanic explosion.

PART I

Examine the ad for a wine cooler. The advertiser uses the word *exotic* to describe the wine. What words offer a clue to the meaning of *exotic*? What idea is the advertiser trying to communicate by using the word *exotic*?

PART II

Draw an ad for a food or drink. Choose one word from the list below that describes your product. Use this word in the ad. Then use other words or phrases in your ad that help the reader understand the meaning of the word you selected from the list. For example, your ad might read like this: "Newport Cherry Soda is delicious. It tastes so good you'll never get enough." The word you selected is *delicious.* The clue words are *tastes so good.*

refreshing	thirst-quenching	convenient
inexpensive	satisfying	pure
crunchy	chewy	healthy
delicious	smooth	